a hermit has no plural

a hermit has no plural

poems by

gabor g gyukics

Singing Bone Press 2015

Acknowledgments

The author extends thanks to the editors of the following
publications where some of these poems have previously
appeared:
Adobe Anthology, Arabesques Review, Big Bridge, Black Buz-
zard Review, Brooklyn Review, Cafe Review, Cream City Re-
view, Cups, East and West Literary Quarterly, Edgar Allen Poet
Journal, Estuary, Foolscape (United Kingdom), Fragrance, Fu-
ture Earth Magazine, Ginosko, Huffington Post, Hunger, In Our
Own Words Anthology, Lost and Found, MadHat Lit., Margutte
(Italy), New Press Literary Quarterly, Nexus, Night, Phati'tude,
Plaza (Japan), Poetry Repair Shop, Salonika, Rampike (Canada),
Stranger at Home Anthology, The Southeast Review, Tight, To
Topos, Untamed Ink, Yellow Medicine

Cover drawing © by Kamilla Gyukics
Cover design © by Réka Nemere
Back cover photo of the author © by Erika Pereszlényi

www.singingbonepress.com
ISBN 978-0-933439-05-4

I am the janitor of the soul

K. Curtis Lyle

poetry is an unintended, sensual manifestation of incessant thinking

ggg

Works by Gabor G Gyukics

Poetry

Utcai Előadás, in Hungarian

Last Smile, English-Hungarian,

A remete többes száma, in Hungarian

versKÉPzelet, poems and writings on art in Hungarian and 22 works by 20 contemporary fine artists

Lepkék vitrinben, in Hungarian

kié ez az arc, in Hungarian

Selected Poetry of Gabor Gyukics in Bulgarian, translated by Stefka Hrusanova,

Prose

Kisfa galeri «socio-horror», in Hungarian

Poetry Translations to English (with Michael Castro)

Swimming in the Ground, Contemporary Hungarian Poetry Anthology

Gypsy Drill, Poems of Attila Balogh, Hungarian edition

A Transparent Lion. Selected poetry of Attila József

Terrenum (The Place of Time), poetry and art by Adam Gall, Hungarian

My God, How Many Mistakes I've Made, Selected poetry of Endre Kukorelly

Poetry Translations to Hungarian

Half-Naked Muse / Félmeztelen múzsa, Contemporary American Poetry Anthology, bi-lingual, Magyar

Átkelés, Contemporary American Poetry Anthology,

Cornucopion-Bőségszaru, selected poetry of Ira Cohen

A szem önéletrajza, selected poetry of Paul Auster,

Nagy-Kis Madár, selected poetry of Jim Northrup

Recording

Sand Snail, poetry in English, Frogpond Productions, Music by Mark Deutsch

Table of Contents

Preface

Gábor G Gyukics is one of the most peculiar figures of Hungarian literary life. He is a poet who is migrating through countries and languages. He stands alone, quite without echoes in the relatively closed tradition of Hungarian poetry. This is partly because, although he began to write poems in Hungarian, he was not living in Hungary.

The features of his art were shaped during his one and half decades spent as a political refugee living in America, far away from developments in Hungary during this period. He left Hungary in 1986 and after two years in the Netherlands he settled in America-- or more exactly he migrated in America, since he spent several years, weeks or just days in different places—years in San Francisco and Brooklyn with many briefer stops in between.

American English became his second poetic language, so his poetic image has been shaped much more by the traditions of American beat and jazz poets he felt kinship with than literary memories brought from his native Hungary. The structure of his free poems evokes Ezra Pound's vorticism, which assigns a special status to poetic image. According to this concept, the "image" is essentially a special moment, when an "external and objective thing is transformed into something or penetrates something, which is internal and subjective." These haiku-like image-moments are placing ordinary objects, things in refraction, depriving them of their familiarity, but giving them a unique freshness.

Orsolya Rákai

in vain

with my left hand on probation
I'm looking for my father
and my mother
in my pocket
I drag them out
and put them into
my other pocket
yet they climb back
they don't like the climate

about to decide
az elhatározás kezdete

through the interfacial
hair-tiny crack
of the locked train window
blown in snow pellets
freeze an iced relief
on the windowsill

the rushing train
scares a heron away
from the iced sedge marsh
along the tracks

a raven chases off
a pair of turtle doves
from a pine tree bough
to see the tracks
drilling through the woods

a pine needle punctures the snow
and suffocates in an ice sheath

a magpie is watching all these

this bird is still at home
it wouldn't want to go
where the sky is not the same

az elhatározás kezdete
about to decide

a zárt vonatablak
érintkező
hajszálnyi résén át
az utasfülkébe
jégdaraként fúvódó hó
hideg permettel
fagyaszt domborművet
az ablakperemre

a száguldó vonat
a vágány menti nádas jegéről
elriaszt egy kócsagot

varjú űz el egy vadgalambpárt
hogy a fenyőfaágról
belássa az erdőt
áttörő síneket

fenyőtű veti magát a hóba
és jéghüvelybe fúl

egy szarka nézi mindezt

még itthon van
nem kíván menni oda
ahol más az ég

the noontide and the chemist
a déli dagály és a kémikus

the funnel of a once to come quizzical noontide
edged itself to the lung-colored branches of ancient trees

a subtle chemist surprised the seashore crowd by
burning himself and becoming the subject of his
own chemistry as he was washed away

the residue didn't register anywhere
only a saw-toothed shadow of a scapula was seen
later under a sinister cliff side

a déli dagály és a kémikus
the noontide and the chemist

A periodikusan visszatérő, kötekedő Déli Dagály tölcsére
Az ősi fák tüdőszín lombjai közé ékelődött

Az éles eszű Kémikus meglepte a tengerparti tömeget
Elégette magát és saját tudományának tárgyává változott
Miközben elmosta a visszavonuló áradat

Maradványait mindmáig nem vetette partra a tenger
Az idő múlásával csak egy lapockacsont fűrészfogú árnya
Vált láthatóvá a fenyegető parti sziklák alatt

cemetery at River Savannah
temető a Savannah folyónál

leaning to the oyster brick fence
watching
as ants order ants to labor
you seem to perceive
whips in their forearms

you won't talk about the place
you 've visited in your dream
to anyone

with prewritten answers
you ignore the questioners

you smooth your forehead
the peeling of your skin
is wind blown dust

under the moonless sky
your shadow walks the sun
to the other side

temető a Savannah folyónál
cemetery at River Savannah

osztrigakagylóból épült kerítésnek támaszkodsz
nézed
amint a temető füvetlen részén
hangya dolgoztat hangyát
látni véled mellső lábai között
a lótetű karmaiból készült ostort

nem mutatod meg senkinek
ezt az álmodban látott helyet
előre megírt válaszokkal
veszed a kérdezőt semmibe

végigsimítod homlokod
hámló bőröd szél mozgatta por

a holdtalan ég alól
árnyékod elkíséri a napot
a folyó másik oldalára

chairs
székek

these chairs should be rearranged
    she said
who would do that
    I said
you
    came her answer
    as she sat
    I moved the other chair close to hers

székek
chairs

át kellene rendezni a székeket
szólt a lány
ki rendezze át
kérdeztem
te
válaszolt
és leült
széke mellé helyeztem székemet

abide

abate to jay walk through this cut off street
where around the corner
assigned agents hunker in the mist
judging your move incongruous
in their inner boredom

you ignore the zealous civil servants
fooling them by flying above the lanes
with your cloud stretching wings
dismissing their concerns
you cross over
landing in the center of this
privately owned neighborhood
paying a visit to no one specific

I'm not here you only imagine me

I need enough hooks to hang my words on
I am hospitable to fleas
and once
where the air was caged
I was an untasted fruit
now
I carry false papers to cross borders
with the one I used to laugh with
I can hardly keep up with her slowness
the papers contain words
that used to be constipated

only the shadow of snow
was able to perceive
what they held inside:

acquisitions, gallivanting, consignment,
humidity, acceleration, reception,
or a wish
that whatever you hope to turn around was going to turn
around –

the poison on your fingertips
seeps into me
around the corner
waiting for the wind
to take us farther away
on its own accord

path

as a vibrant leaf
fallen from a storm beaten tree
the wind rolls me into mould

above the ground ants
below worms
turn me into gold

forge or subdue

a man of deception drove a red car
stolen from a white hearted garage
across the neighborhood of perpetual music,
turned the street corner that vaguely resembled a Middle
Eastern hell
where he had spent years in an area sanctuary,
sneezing purposely to achieve separation
from the goggle eyed alliance of poisonous,
covertly intelligent servicemen of his own country.
now again he unwillingly crossed the line
of sludged sentiment he wished to eliminate
from the archives of his system and
deciphered that he hated those who wanted to have him
and
hated those who were not interested in having him.
after arriving to silence he sat down on an unfamiliar
stoop and
dreamed of a piece of water-jewelry
that the daughter of a pearl diver wore around her neck.

whose face it is

the mirror shows a different picture every day

the flame shooting out from the fireplace
it's counting the new arrivals
the flame of the candle says good bye
to those who are going away

anticipation gathers inside
a butterfly with spread wings
lies on the burning rocky floor

paint rolls off of the wall
the house rises up for
the fresh faced wind
to fly it
to another place

it cares not

a cigarette smoulders with you together
the wind comes in to fetch the smoke
looks around
what else there is to take
but rather it sniffs
shows a grimace
tears a piece off a paper bag
tips over a plastic cup
hits you in the face
pushes the curtain to the side
and
slams the window
after leaving you behind

that is your own

during tail-wind
the headwind
pushes you back
only the motion remains

your body is searching for the gap
your eyes are already behind the wind

the weight of nothing in your head
is a pawn pressed in the corner
you won't meet him ever
but what's waiting

it has nothing to do with …
in memoriam ira cohen

say farewell to all the previous notions
walk among sleeping crocodiles
towards the center of colors
not withstanding the magnetism of mysteries
below the crowds of nothing
under the skies of unnamed entities
along the chords of the infinite circle

with silent lips
with goggled eyes
with storming calmness inside your skull
your defenseless cells lead your invisible steps
across the forbidden zone

yellow fog feeds
your leftover body

script

chairs never place themselves in order
we sit statue erect
there are no gladiolas
in the vase
no wine, no beer bottles
on the table
yet plenty of cigarette smoke
separately
searching for the gaps,
we all drink liqueur,
stand carefully up,
step out to the garden,
the mosquito-net door is ajar,
the wicker chairs squeak after us
when we jump the railing above the gate
stumble on the dirt road
through waist high grassland
crushing weeds, flowers
not bowing to branches
tearing bushes to pieces
towards the river.
If we are not fortunate
we'll get across safely.

stuck in an elevator

two pages remained empty by accident
nocturnal faces change
vanity chimes
endangered species live on
streets with no name
along naked trees
houses with no furnace, no chimney
suicide works unintentionally
it's all the sign of the brain's equilibrium
while a destitute French beauty
smiles before praying and goes
to live approvingly
as soon as she exits
she becomes part of the crowd
an initial cut on the abdomen
oh, darling
the gum is swollen in the mouth
optical green wire stretches from the ankle up
to the skinless hip
its quiet now

enviable death

vestibules without banisters
are as safe
as watches that tumble on the ground
tick-tocking on.
an instant heart failure
is as deadly
as an instant heart failure,
as the trap we erect for ourselves,
as a hole dug by sorrow.
a hole dug by sorrow
fills up as easily
as a hole dug by sorrow.
a hole dug by sorrow
fills up as easily
as a water drum under the gutter,
as a water drum under the gutter.
an instant heart failure
is an enviable death

the snake is back

crestfallen serpent carries her poison
wrenching, lingering around a fair church
stealing priests' dream

the priests are carelessly holding
white gloves and umbrellas
their bare feet flash as they prowl
not thinking while crossing over
to curiously stare at lately acquired pictures
of locals who would never return
to pursue their faith, to persuade each other for
a simple substance which hasn't remained here
only vague attacks
abrupt faints and
peremptory sacrifices

no rain has fallen
no cold air arrived

the snake empties her poison
in the holy water with
paradisial calmness

through doors, windows
she returns and coils up
on her highchair
she is the doctor of
nonsensical illusions
guarding the antidote

between

at day break
the view is glossy whichever way we look
our eyes are covered with a foggy film
naughty barmaids clean drinking glasses
their fingers leave their prints on
when they place them in the cabinet
a tiny dog barks out of a bag
sitting on a girls lap
cheese eaters devour the smoke with every bite
while talking faster and louder
then the sound of the dishwasher
the utensil music
the ice cracking in every drink
and the chattered words that
bind limbs and gage lips
at sundown

vanity chimes in vain

I have a hole in my forehead
ants dug out the socket
crawled inside
created a den for their coquette

before I drove them out
no need for ants to sit by
I thanked them for finding
my third eye

retuning a broken keyboard

silver dirty snow-spots scattered
around on the peaks of the mountains
clear water rain washed the smudged snow
down to the river's throat

the wash off entered the organic system
flew through the pipes, the bowels
some particles oozed inside the vessels
glued themselves to the walls
of all the hiding organs

the rest ran through the programs
of metabolism to be coughed up
by the river's mouth and what remained
of the smutted snow
was spurted out to unsalt
the sea

rendering the view

someone parted the curtains
to have a look at the stereoscopic world
and got crazed immediately
via a suggested attitude of an
offspring of a numberless laboratory
who is setting in thermal dust

this fact is a wild profusion
a nonoccasional confirmation
it is not
the saturation of a Persian turban
during the annual ball of the victims

it is a symptom
a flack
geography
carnage

the entity
who is running all these
is swimming in your hand

blades of fire eaters

the lips of the bathtub
squeezed your bone splintered
fleshy frame
inside the tub's sinkhole
to join hundreds of razorblades
that used to belong to the
tub's previous owner

your body assimilated
with the new environment
in vain for the blades
dissipated the flesh
the bone and all
the organs to become
nourishment of underground
fire eaters who claimed to
have survived sudden
spontaneous combustions
by the tracks below the closed
off subway station that one time
housed pet crocodiles
who were forced to consume
the remaining flakes
of your sometime physical entity

your soul got trapped as well
for it lost its sense of empty space

capitative knowledge

you want to know
what something means
after you have seen it
done it
experienced it

it inordinately
would turn into an allegory

it's not you who is walking
by moving your limbs
it's the earth
under the foot of your sole
that makes you move
on the ominous surface

avoid the slavery of appearances
the counter inductive captions
the attenuated
infective
hyphenated
forgotten alphabets
for it's dangerous
to be named

somewhere between

hooked circles cast shadows
in the center point of haze
to entertain god and the devil
while they are sitting
in a nursery of their choosing
surrounded by antenna sentinels
at the margin of lost simplicity
dolorously lit without gravity
before the parchment of the atmosphere

invisible birds from the ebbing mist
diversify scavenged rendezvous of
repressed promises offered by an
elaborated expressive conception
of an immensely profound entity
on top of a madrone
presenting white flower anchors
in the evening wind
to survive
the tides

wouldn't it be so nice without me

the scattered forces of the apexed sun
is exempt of mortal care

a rising or setting of thermal haze
scroll along the precious atmosphere

it isn't a matter of logistics
it has nothing to do with any
human who might be
the aim of any innuendo

it is the doing of a lame
seamless
evanescent
thimbleman
who gets done on his four
to crawl, shuffle, rig and weave a first rate yarn

hoping to please and alter the mind
of the spoiled one
who is roaming in ghost light
without any previous engagement

transparent ink

stains the dirty rind of a
resin hat of a
man standing by the
train's window in a
land
where the air is
not yet futile
back in the last times
when hand rolled cigarette smoke
blew out of the fissures of
wooden wheeled carriages

the man inhales
deep
keeps the smoke down
exhales
the smoke shivers
mingles with the air
when
an escaped piece of
breeze hits the man's face

he feels fear gathering
in his mouth

the shadow and the trigger

the ventilator relentlessly spun above the bar
the edge of its blade looked like
desperately escaping hungry wings of a bat
that's what he saw
while sipping his beer
in Dressel's, his favorite St. Louis bar
in the wooden framed mirror
hanging on the opposite wall

his plane just flew in from Brooklyn
he slept until the end of the flight
when he began following the plane's shadow
with his eyes

a small dot crossing over well tended fields below
while landing he watched the shadow grow bigger
mightier while approaching the plane
and when the throbbing silvery machine
hit the ground
the shadow joined it
silently, comfortingly
the way a finger joins the trigger

what is still hiding there

in the very center of a compound
in an immediate connection
I crack apertures one after another
until I reach one side of it
here the wall is thicker
practically impervious
uniting from nothing
I can only peek out
through the imperceptible tiny rift
to see

at the airport

you had no tears
but glued a half smile
on your face
kept yourself busy
with this and that
stared at my suitcase
when you found nothing else around
to touch
but me

this yellow raglan sleeve coat
looks good on you
I said
instead of saying
I'll be back

you took your coat off and
put it in your bag

fly

a sad bird froze to the neighbor's windshield.
its snow stuffed body
hail picking beak
and sickle stiff claws
shattered the safety glass
into non-recyclable trash.
the swearing neighbor
grabbed the ice-winged carcass
broke it in half
gathered the pieces
and threw them up to the winter air.
Fly! - he screamed
Fly! - he screamed raging cold-blooded
at the scene of the scheme
not seeing
as the two half birds came to life
rose to fall
one winged
wedged
into his reddening eyes

the promise of pain is the language of cabbala

yet I want to release it.
I tried massage,
tigerbalm,
painkillers,
stopped drinking wine,
drank only water and tea,
yet the thousand faces of surprised pain
didn't cease to die off,
still it was like glass-shards.
then I figured,
if I reach inside the pain
and displace it to a nonfunctional object,
like a mug,
and break it to pieces,
it stops lingering,
fades away,
 becomes someone else's
 pain.

chrysalis

a diabolically consolidated wasp's nest with a
woman as its resilient keeper was found in the
same woman's vertebrae during autopsy,
the coroner seemed bathetic as he turgidly
drew his initials on the side of the nest
in the rancid spine line to ensure his first right
to this bouncing discovery.

the woman's puffed up face showed aversion
regarding the intrusion into her cagey body,
she was inclined to diminish the coroner's derogatory
invasion for she had been nurturing these
ferocious inhabitants of her nest with
complimentary attention, with
utter persuasion to let them maintain their
own proliferation by overlooking
flowers in dewy cemeteries,
jiving tactile grave diggers as the primary goal of exist-
ence.

now, at present the woman's bony shell
is laid out in the morgue, with the
abandoned nest inside her waiting for the
final taxidermy.

while you were around
          for michael castro

the morning wind
swallowed your words
aimed at me
on the top of Monks Mound

your escaping thoughts
were stammered into my ears
by a gesticulating Chinese man
later that afternoon

in the midst of rush hour traffic
substituting an invisible pow-wow
in front of the Vietnamese fish stall
on Olive Boulevard in St. Louis,

upon the arrival of your words
I looked inside the man's eyes
to disappear behind his iris

tale

an old Ojibwa
the grandfather of numerous children
walks the land that was assigned to his tribe
every day

he follows the paths of animals
watches the wild rice to ear in the lake
the wing-strikes of the birds
strokes the crust of the maple
spears walleye at night
hunts moose in the woods
rests in his sweat lodge

one day
in a shallow crevice
he found a nugget
streaked with gold

he walked it to the depth of the woods
and dug a hole for it

totem

the skyscrapers in the streets
named after native tribes
are not occupied by orchid hunters
rather by alpine window cleaners
and security officers
who became the twelve intervals of the scale

occasionally
the breathing of invisible Indian People
is heard
and their scent of earth
can be sensed
in the cities

adjustment to the environment

it's hot,
I drink a shot to become hotter,
I don't feel like drinking tea,
it's said that in Asia,
during the hot season,
people drink hot liquid to adjust their bodies,
to the outside temperature,
it's not my reason,
I want to burn from inside
not to decompose,
but to be absorbed, to disappear with no trace,
simply,
inconspicuously,
but only my stomach turns itself on,
when I sit in the loo my nose is always running,
my system draws a parallel between two actions,
hot shower, another shot,
and out to the heat,
the shadow has already lost its function,
every woman is pregnant this morning

lust

diseased flies copulate on my pastry

greeks

gone
the greeks
you say
stone willow
pebble weeps
rock cradle
erect column
time is rain

that what...

I am a sheet of metal on edge
carousel-scream
derailed train
thrown away letter
or only a figure
door slam
boiled over milk
bent spine
dry riverbed
and not that

other people's images

staggering, flashing sirens cut your thoughts in half
the zipper broke on your leotard revealing virgin fingertips
the blood ran out of them when they were severed from
your hands
now they are displayed in a secondhand gallery for every-
one's view
the TV is running in the closet behind drawn curtains
entertaining ants, roaches and a cat whose tail was
chopped off
by a slammed door
the toilet bowl is clogged up with carelessly devoured
nourishment
torn family photos soak in the bathtub's rusty water
your eyes are someone's mirror across the ocean
your face is a lost article in my brain
your thighs are a dream of runaway teenagers
your nipples are in your own mouth
your knees are touching the parquet
shots of bourbon rumble through your heart
smoke gathers in your lungs
stretched out arms of a yesterday paper-covered body grab
your legs
saving you from stepping on quicksand
rag-dolls embrace your hips
it's a jerking pleasure
it's the coldest time of the night
a naked kiss lands on your lips
I enter your mind
I live in your head

still life in color

the spring sun shines through the dirty rainbow curtain
bringing warmth to the cold room
the outside cool remains untouched
the sun doesn't care to warm it up
the november air of april mingles
with thrown away beer cans, candy wrappers
and shit stained newspapers on the pavement
the sand colored window glass is licked clean by a rusty
cat
as the red girl laughs her teeth out of her immigrant
kissed mouth
volatile sheet rock drops copulate with a matted hair lock
on the mattress
half-read books lie scattered on the smirking shelves
while undaunted cigarette smoke burdens the eyes of the
broken tenants midway out the door
trousers in one hand
futile red wine bottles in the other
dashboard silence grays the room
I'm stuck in the air facing the whitewashed ceiling
levitating
waiting for a bee-sting to set me loose

dream that never happened

white, naked body breathes on the ground
pure, rough, black surroundings
fable music vibrates through
while the little, white, nude girl lies
in the bleakness
a pale feather flutters by
they don't know each other
the whitewashed girl and the feather
they both would like to speak to someone

in the frozen silence
a sword
slices the feather into snowflakes
like a guillotine
separates the white head
from the white body

her open eyes
now
reflect unexpected alleviation

long walk
for ira cohen

the numbers on his telephone
disappeared from too much dialing.
it was cold outside,
he put his pants on, his shoes,
a shirt, a cloak,
a scarf around his neck,
held a hat in his hand.
he left to visit his acquaintances

checking out of life

a hand releases the clump of hair of a young woman
from a half open window
while she is reading a book on enlightenment
and emptying her bowels in the bathroom
of an Upper West Side condo on the 8th floor
filled with photographs
taken by a man who believed
 that dreamlessness equals insanity.
the woman leaves her bathroom
cleansed of all burden
cover every mirror when they die.

twins

a freighter carrying suicidal twins
anchored on the Adriatic
close to an Italian port

they went ashore
and one of them
got stoned

the act was cheered
by the village idiot

the twin
still alive
swam back to the boat
and lit a smoke.

blade in fashion

wearing a transparent gown
she crossed the threshold
approaching the guillotine
with shorn hair
with red scarf around her neck
with an easy walk
she passed the executioner
stepped off the podium
leaving bloody footsteps
on the cobble stone of the
ctagonal square
sunk into the steaming clouds
of the mobs perspiration
making her entrance in the
carnage of the 21st century

erasable street signs

I brushed a palm against a silver cigarette case,
it bent, it curved feeling the touch,
a hollow measure.

a pebble tumbled out of a corner
to find the rain

like my mother
who prays everywhere,
to save her son,
to find his lost notebook,
just to loose it again
around...

forgery

a dead man was kept in ice for over a year
because of lack of funding
by a lazy host.
his eyes want to sleep
but the head is no pillow.

pyramidal structures built from boxes
packed with olives
are scattered around the cemetery
a film rolls by the architects.
a goat instinctively grazes particles
at the gas station near by.
the dead man lost his spurs riding a wooden horse
while he was still alive.
his coffin is being used by someone else.

designated areas

missed the train
got rained on
got lost
to avoid us
the stars gathered at the most distant point of the sky
saw frozen laundry on a rope
stretched between two trees
as we walked by a Canadian village
a well-designated area
riding in a shabby truck
we vanished in the city
where wire nets slung between metal poles
holding up falling objects
from newly built high-rises
"take your mask off before entering"
said a sign welded on the door
of a liquor store
as we walked in
we checked and
secured
our camouflage

reflection of the dark

there was a blue carrot on the Savoy
like a fish
or the shadow of a ring
the room was full of mosquitoes
"Are you still alive?" asked Emperor Caracalla
I forgot to smile
took some steps slightly
it was dark in the streets
god closed his eyes
looked like a jovial tiger
as he spread his sickness on earth
I don't say anything
just listen to your silence
I dreamt that an elephant stole my nickname
the room darkened as well
years passed away
where they disappeared I don't know
someone knocked on the door
opened it
more
darkness

when they found me dead on Duke Ellington
Boulevard

when they found me dead
I was waiting for the angels of heaven and hell
to take my soul to
where ever they wished to store it
they didn't come
only an nypd cop and a coroner came
leaning casually above me
I grabbed the two men and freed their souls
their limp bodies calmly fell upon me

leaving…

snow-patched roofs remain behind
mud tainted windows
trash laden streets, squares

wine smudged tablecloths
greasy plates, bowls

ash stained undershirts
dirty bedsheets

postcard loaded
bench appears

waiting for the wind

scavenger

staring at good looking butts
pick a few up
stack them on empty
cigarette packs
enjoy them
when
got some matches

it

we aren't printed matter
we don't fade
or if we do
we are restored
either before
or after
it happened

snail on ice

In a cold room, in a cold bed, under a cold blanket
the body is cold
the light is cold, the night is cold, the moon is cold
the grass and the tree are cold
the earth is cold, its smell is cold
the sun is cold, the breath is cold under the cold water
the sky is cold, the cloud is cold, the flashlight is cold
the meat is cold in the cold soup
the girl is cold, the desire is cold
the word flags
cold wedged beneath the stone
the blood is cold, the mind is cold
the music is cold, the picture is cold, the hieroglyph is cold
the hot tea is cold
the flower is cold, the bird is cold, the bee is cold
the mayfly is cold
in the cold, cold sculpture stopped movement
the sweltering heat is cold, the time is cold, the
brain is cold
the beggar is cold, his eyes are cold
cold running through my throat
my lungs are cold and tremble
my legs are cold and I can't go
in the cold I stand lying or I lie standing
I don't know in the cold
in the cold
everything
is

About the author

Gabor G Gyukics (b. 1958 in Budapest) Hungarian-American poet, literary translator. He spent two years in Holland before moving to the United States where he had lived between 1988-2002. At present he resides in the isle of Csepel in Budapest, Hungary. He is the author of five books of original poetry, one book of original prose and ten books of poetry translations including the work of Attila József.

His poetic works and translations have been published in magazines and anthologies in English, Hungarian and other languages worldwide. He received the Füst Milán translator prize in 1999, the National Cultural Foundation grant in 2007 and the 2012 Salvatore Quasimodo special prize for poetry. Thanks to an Arts Link grant, he had established an open mike and jazz poetry series within Hungary in 1999.

He is a member of the Belletrist Association of Hungary and the Hungarian Translators Association. At present he is editing and translating the poetic works of North American Indigenous poets for an anthology to be published in Hungarian.